This book records the early life of Kitten ....

This book is dedicated to all the dear
little pet kittens in the world.
Long may they purr in peace and happiness.

KITTEN RECORD BOOK

by Barbara Hayes
Illustrations by Douglas Hall

Published in 1988 by
Brian Trodd Publishing House Ltd
27 Swinton Street, London WC1

©Brian Trodd Publishing House Ltd 1988

All rights reserved. No part of this book
may be reproduced or utilised in any form
or by any means, electronic or
mechanical, including photocopying,
recording, or by any information storage
and retrieval system, without permission
in writing from the publisher.

ISBN 1 85361 018 6

Printed in Hong Kong

CONTENTS

Important Kitten Information	8-9
First Meeting	10
Other Cats and Kittens	11
Coming Home Day	12
Photographs or Drawings	13-15
Growth Chart	16
Height Chart for Children in the Family	17
Medical Record	18
Playing at Pets' Hospital	19
Favourite Food	20
Food Dishes	21
Photographs	22-23
Kitten's Toys	24-25
Sleeping Places	26
Kitten's Weight	27
Learning to Go Outdoors	28
Learning to Use a Cat Flap	29
Teething	30
Photographs	31
Other Pets in the House	32
Pets Who Live Nearby	33
Kitten Talk	34
Kitten Understanding	35
Kitten Funtime	36
Photographs	37
Kitten Rainy Afternoon Story	38-42
Brushing and Grooming	43
Holidays and Visits	44
Christmas Days	45
Birthdays	46
Who Loves Kitten	47

IMPORTANT KITTEN INFORMATION

Your kitten's name and address are important. They can also change. On this page you can keep a record of your kitten's pedigree name, the name you use every day and any other pet names you may give to your little friend. There are also spaces for writing your kitten's home address and any changes of address which may take place. If you have not been learning to write for very long, perhaps a kind grown-up will help you with any difficult words.

Date..

Kitten's pedigree name ....

Kitten's everyday name..

Kitten's pet name..

Kitten's address ....

Date..

Kitten's pet name if different from above...

Some kittens come from expensive, pedigree families.
Here is a page where you can keep a record of all the important
family history of your pet.

Breed of kitten..

Name of mother...

Name of father ....

Name of breeder...

Address where Kitten was born..

....

Names of any prizewinning or important members of Kitten's family ....

....

What prizes did they win?..

....

....

What relation were these prize winners to Kitten? e.g. Grandma?.......................

Grandpa? Uncle? Auntie? Cousin?..

Details of any registration of pedigree..

....

Where are any registration certificates kept? e.g. in an envelope clipped in at the

end of this book..

FIRST MEETING

When a family decides to buy a kitten, a visit is usually paid to the place where the kitten is born. The mother cat and the litter of kittens are inspected and one of the sweet little bundles of fur is chosen as the pet the family will love. Kittens do not usually leave their mothers until they are between three and four months old, but the visit to choose the kitten can take place much earlier. This page is where you can record what happened when you or someone from your family first saw your future pet.

Date of first meeting..

Which family members went to first meeting?..

Did they see the mother cat? ....

If so what was her name? ....

Did they see the father cat? ....

If so what was his name? ....

Did they see the brother and sister kittens? ....

Who chose your pet kitten? ....

Was your kitten chosen because it was friendly?..

pretty? ....

lively?..

lovable?..

OTHER CATS AND KITTENS

There are many types of cats and kittens in the world. There are long-haired and short-haired, domestic cats and wild cats, Persians and Angoras, tabby cats, Manx cats with no tails, black cats and silvery Chinchilla cats, blue cats and Siamese cats, tortoiseshell cats and white cats. Even lions and tigers are members of the cat family.

Think about all these cats and then write down which breed of

kitten you would like to own if you had the choice ....

But your own pet is nicest of all, isn't it? ....

....

COMING HOME DAY: KITTEN INFORMATION

At last the great day arrives when the kitten can leave its mother and come to live with you in its new home. As the months go by, it is so easy to forget what kitten was like when he or she was tiny. This page will help you to remember.

Date when kitten arrived home ....

Age of kitten ....

Colour of kitten ....

Colour of kitten's eyes ....

How did kitten travel home? ....

By car? ....

By train? ....

By boat? ....

By bus? ....

By walking? ....

Did kitten seem to like his new home? ....

PHOTOGRAPHS or DRAWINGS

If you have any photographs of Kitten when he or she was little, ask if you may fix them on this page. If you have no photographs, ask if you may draw pictures of Kitten. If you are not good at drawing, perhaps Mummy or some other kind grown-up will draw a picture of Kitten for you.

COMING HOME DAY: ALL ABOUT YOU AND THE FAMILY

Not only Kitten changes from week to week. You and your family change too. This page will help you to remember how things were on the day that kitten arrived.

How many children were living in the house when Kitten arrived home?..........

What were their names? ....

How old were they? ....

How many grown-ups were living in the house when Kitten arrived home?....

What were their names? ....

Who stroked Kitten on his first day at home?...

Who fed Kitten on his first day at home? ....

....

Was home a house or a flat or something else?..

Was home in the town or in the country?..

Was the weather sunny?.......warm?..........wet?........cold?..

PHOTOGRAPHS or DRAWINGS

If you have any photographs of yourself or any other members of your family, ask if you may fix them here. If you have no photographs, ask if you may draw pictures instead.

GROWTH CHART

Growing bigger every month is a sign of a healthy kitten. Here is a chart on which you can keep a record of how your fluffy little pet is eating his way to becoming a big, strong cat. Use a ruler or tape measure to measure your kitten's length from nose tip to tail tip. You will have to be quick because kittens do not like standing still. Do not hurt Kitten by pulling him into line. If he does not want to be measured, leave him in peace. Instead why not measure your own height for the chart on the opposite page? Ask Mummy or Daddy to measure Kitten later on.

Here   to   Here

HEIGHT CHART FOR CHILDREN IN THE FAMILY

Kittens are not the only creatures which grow. Good children who eat up their proper meals grow too. If you keep a monthly record of your height, you can see who is growing more, you or the kitten. If there is more than one child in the family use a different coloured crayon for recording the height of each child. Make a note at the bottom of the page of which colour is for which little person. In a month it is easy to forget whose colour is which.

MEDICAL RECORD

This is a very important page. If your dear little pet is taken ill, which we hope will never happen, you will probably take him to see a cat doctor called a veterinary surgeon, or 'vet' for short. The vet will want to know if the kitten has ever been ill before and what injections he has been given. Show what a good pet owner you are by making a record of everything a vet may want to know.

	Type	Date	By whom
Injections given to Kitten			
Any other medical treatment			
Kitten's illnesses and their dates			

Try to keep this page filled up to date. Then you will really deserve for the vet to say to you: 'WELL DONE!'

PLAYING AT PETS' HOSPITAL

Perhaps you will be a 'vet' one day and care for the pets of other people. You could start your training now by playing at Pets' Hospitals. Remember always play with TOY Animals. NEVER PLAY HOSPITALS WITH REAL ANIMALS. Real animals do not like being pulled about and bandaged.

When you are ready to play hospitals, wash your own hands and put on a clean pinafore, apron or doctor's or nurse's outfit if you have one. Ask Mummy if she has any clean old towels you may use. If you have a doll's bed or toy shopping baskets or old shopping baskets Mummy lets you play with, put them all in a row.

Then look at your TOYS. Perhaps one of them has an upset stomach. The treatment for this is to be put in a clean, warm basket and wrapped round with an old towel. Put a little water in a saucer nearby for the toy to drink if it wishes, but give it no food until it feels better.

If one of the TOYS has hurt its foot, bathe the foot carefully with real or pretend water. Wrap a bandage round it and put the toy to rest in a basket or little bed.

If you think any of the TOYS have colds, wrap them up warm, put them in a basket or little bed, wipe their noses often and give them little titbits to eat or drink when they seem hungry.

When you have finished playing, tidy everything away and you will be well on the way to learning to be a fine vet.

FAVOURITE FOOD

Kittens like different sorts of food at different ages. Here is a page on which you can record your kitten's favourite foods and make a list of who gives them to him.

Kitten's favourite foods at three months ....

....

Kitten's favourite foods at six months ....

....

Kitten's favourite foods at nine months ....

....

Kittens's favourite foods at one year old ....

....

Who gives kitten his meals? Write down the names of everyone who has

ever given a meal to Kitten ....

....

....

....

....

....

....

FOOD DISHES

Does Kitten have a water dish?..

If so would you like to draw a picture of it here?..

Does Kitten have a food dish?...

If so would you like to draw a picture of it here?..

Does Kitten have a milk dish?...

If so would you like to draw a picture of it here?..

Does Kitten ever try to take food which belongs to someone else?....................

Whose food?..

Does anyone ever give Kitten tit-bits between meals?..

What are Kitten's favourite tit-bits?..

....

....

....

PHOTOGRAPHS

If you have any photographs of Kitten, ask if you may fix them here.
At the side of the photographs write the date on which they were
taken. If you can remember, write the name of
the person who took the photographs.

PHOTOGRAPHS or DRAWINGS or SCRAP PICTURES

Here is another page for photographs of Kitten or any other members of the family. If you have no photographs, ask if you may draw pictures. Perhaps you like to cut out pictures of kittens from magazines. If you do, here is a good place to stick them, if Mummy agrees.

KITTEN'S TOYS

Like children, kittens enjoy playing with toys. Here is a list of good toys for Kitten to play with. Answer yes or no if your kitten has ever played with any of them.

Good Toys: Has your kitten ever played with a ball?..

Has your kitten ever played with a cotton reel hung on a string?.......................

Has your kitten ever played with a toy mouse? ....

Has your kitten ever played with a scratching log?..

Has your kitten ever played jumping in and out of a cardboard box?...............

KITTEN'S TOYS

Sometimes kittens play with things they should not touch. Here is a list of naughty toys. Answer yes or no if your kitten has ever played with any of them.

Naughty Toys: Has your kitten ever played running up the curtains?................

Has your kitten ever played making a bed on someone's best woolly sweater?..

Has your kitten ever played with today's newspaper?...

SLEEPING PLACES

Kittens and cats spend a lot of time sleeping. Here is a page on which you can record the changing sleeping habits of your pet.

In which room does Kitten sleep at night at 3 months old?..................................

In which room does Kitten sleep at night at 6 months old?..................................

In which room does Kitten sleep at night at 9 months old?..................................

In which room does Kitten sleep at night at one year old?..................................

Does Kitten sleep in a basket or a box?..

Where does Kitten sleep in the daytime?...

Some kittens sleep for 16 hours a day. How many hours do you think your kitten sleeps for at 3 months?........at 6 months?..........at 9 months........at one year old?...........

At 3 months	At 6 months	At 9 months	At 1 year

KITTEN'S WEIGHT

Kitten's weight is important. However persuading Kitten to sit still on the bathroom scales is not easy. If you or a grown-up are clever enough to take Kitten's weight, here is a chart on which you can record it.

	At 3 months	At 6 months	At 9 months	At 1 year
Kitten's Weight				
Who weighed Kitten				
Who wrote the weight				

LEARNING TO GO OUTDOORS

Kittens and cats like to prowl about on their own. They can climb fences and jump over gates. You do not want your new little pet to get lost so he has to be taught to know his own house and garden. However at last the great day will come when you let Kitten into the garden on his own.

When did Kitten first go out alone?..

Did he stay in the garden? ....

Did he climb the fence and try to wander off?..

Did he try to slip under the gate?..

Did he chase the birds? ....

Did he meet any other cats or kittens? ....

Did he enjoy his outing?..

LEARNING TO USE A CAT FLAP

As he grows older, Kitten will want to go in and out of the house as he wishes. This is when he will appreciate a cat flap, although at first he may not know what it is.

How old was Kitten when you fitted a cat flap for him? ....

Did he know what it was? ....

Did you have to push him through it to show him how to use it? ....

How long did it take Kitten to learn to use the cat flap properly? ....

Do other cats try to use the cat flap? ....

Cats are clean animals. With the help of the cat flap, a kitten should be quite clean in the house. Is your kitten clean indoors? ....

TEETHING

Just like human beings, cats have milk teeth, which they shed in order to make room for their grown-up teeth.

When did your kitten start losing its milk teeth? ....

Did you find any little teeth lying about the house? ....

How old was Kitten when he had all his grown-up teeth? ....

Or does no one dare to look into Kitten's mouth to see? ....

Do you have any grown-up teeth? ....

If there are other children in the family, do they have any grown-up teeth? ...

How many grown-up teeth altogether for all the children? ....

PHOTOGRAPHS

Here is another page on which you may fix photographs or make drawings of your kitten or other members of the family.

OTHER PETS IN THE HOUSE

Kitten may not be the only pet in the house. Here is a page on which you can write the names and type of animal of any other pets. Perhaps you have a dog, or a canary or some fish. Write all the details here.

PETS WHO LIVE NEARBY

The people who live nearby to you may have pets. Perhaps one home has a big guard dog, or another may have a pony in a meadow. There may be cats who are friendly with your kitten or there may be others which are always looking for fights. Here is a space where you can write the names of the pets who live near to you. If you do not know how to write their names, you could draw little pictures instead.

KITTEN TALK

Kittens and cats cannot talk in the way humans do, but they make many different sorts of sounds. They purr, squeak, hiss, yowl and miaow. The big members of the cat family, like lions and tigers, also roar in very loud voices. Here is a page where you can record the different sounds Kitten has learned to make.

Can Kitten purr? ....

Can Kitten squeak? ....

Can Kitten hiss? ....

Can Kitten yowl? ....

Can Kitten miaow? ....

Can Kitten roar? ....

If he does, you are in trouble. You must have bought
a lion or tiger by mistake.

KITTEN UNDERSTANDING:

Although your kitten does not speak human language, he will soon learn to understand some human words. Hopefully he will learn the meaning of 'no' and 'yes'. Without doubt he will soon know what you mean when you call 'dinner'. Here is a space in which you can write the words which your kitten understands.

Kittens usually understand some people better than others. If you and Mummy are with kitten much of the time, he will take more notice of you, than of someone he does not see often. Here is a space where you may make a list of the people Kitten understands best.

....

....

....

....

....

....

....

....

....

....

KITTEN FUNTIME

Because they live with human beings, kittens learn to like things they would never see in a wild life. Some kittens like watching television. Some like listening to music on the radio. Some like to answer the telephone. Some like sitting with children and listening to stories. Some even like scrabbling about inside paper bags. What unusual things does your kitten like to do?

Does Kitten watch television?..

Does Kitten listen to the radio?...

Does Kitten answer the telephone?..

Does Kitten like listening to stories?...

Does Kitten like playing with paper bags?...

What else does Kitten like to do?...

PHOTOGRAPHS

Here is more space for photographs of your dear little pet.

KITTEN RAINY AFTERNOON STORY

This is a story for kittens and for all those who love kittens. It can be read at any time, but is especially suitable for reading on rainy afternoons when no one can go out to play.

Once upon a time little Kimmy Kitten was born on a farm in the country. Kimmy had two brothers and one sister. For two or three months life was wonderful. Mummy Cat supplied plenty of warm milk for the kittens to drink. Later on the farmer's wife put down saucers of delicious food for the kittens and Mummy Cat to eat. Mummy Cat taught her babies how to keep themselves clean and neat, how to climb trees and fences safely and how to hunt and chase away mice and birds from the farm. When Kimmy Kitten needed playmates, there were always her brothers and sister to romp with.

Every day a boy called Johnny came to work at the farm. He seemed to like Kimmy Kitten. Every day he gave her a stroke and a pat and he used to say to the farmer's wife: "We need a kitten at our cottage. My sister

Mary says she has seen signs of mice near the kitchen door. We need a cat in the house to stop the mice coming inside and nibbling at our food."

The farmer's wife would smile at Johnny, who was a good honest worker, and she would say: "Well, you seem to like young Kimmy. When the time is right I will give her to you and she can live with you and Mary at the cottage."

Kimmy was horrified.

"I am very happy here," she thought. "I don't want to leave Mummy Cat, who gives me delicious warm milk. I don't want to leave my brothers and sister, who are such fun to play with."

For a while Kimmy Kitten tried to avoid Johnny, the hard-working farmer's boy. However Johnny was such a cheery young fellow and tickled Kimmy so nicely behind the ears, that she could not help liking him.

"But I won't let the farmer's wife give me to Johnny," thought Kimmy. "I will stay with Mummy Cat and the other kittens on this farm for ever."

Then strange things started to happen. Mummy Cat did not seem to have so much nice warm milk to give away. She started cuffing her kittens round the ears when they asked for a drink.

"Don't bother me!" she would miaow. "I have done enough for you. You are growing big enough to look after yourselves."

After several days of this Kimmy and the others had to ask the farmer's wife for food or hunt for their own. And somehow the other kittens were not as friendly as they used to be. They were growing larger. When Kimmy tried to play with one of her brothers or her sister, she found they had become quite rough. What used to be a playful little pat with a paw had become a fearsome little punch. OUCH!

Kimmy stopped trying to play with the other kittens any more. In any case, with all the searching for food she had to do, there was little time for play.

"What is the world coming to?" thought Kimmy. "Why did things have to change? I am not happy at the farm any more."

Then suddenly Kimmy thought of Johnny the farmer's boy. He still came to work at the farm every day and he still made a favourite of Kimmy and stroked her back and tickled behind her ears. Perhaps going with Johnny to live at the cottage with him and his sister, Mary, would not be so bad after all.

When Kimmy Kitten was three and a half months old, the farmer's wife said to Johnny: "The time is right. Tell your sister Mary to get a nice warm bed and feeding bowls ready for Kimmy and tomorrow you may take her home with you."

Kimmy Kitten was delighted. By this time Mother Cat would have nothing to do with her at all and her brothers and sister did nothing but quarrel with her over food.

"I see that I am growing up," purred Kimmy to herself, "and a home of my own is what I need."

The next day when Johnny had finished his work, Kimmy Kitten was waiting for him by the farmhouse door. She did not need to be given to him. She jumped up into his arms and rubbed her cheeks against his jacket.

So Johnny took Kimmy Kitten home to his sister Mary, who loved her at once. Kimmy settled into the cottage very happily and was a wonderful pet for years. No mice dared set a foot indoors while Kimmy was on guard.

And that is the way with all kittens. When the time is right they need to leave Mother Cat and the other kittens and go to a new home of their own. That is why your own kitten was so happy to come to live with you.

BRUSHING AND GROOMING

Cats and kittens are clean animals. However a little extra care from their owners always helps to keep pets in good condition. Kittens should be brushed and combed regularly, especially the long-haired breeds. It is easy to hurt a cat by tugging at its hair, so perhaps grooming is a task better left to grown-ups or bigger children. Smaller members of the family who wish to help could perhaps lend a hand with brushing out kitten's basket or box, or washing his blanket and hanging it on the washing line.

Here are pictures of brushes, combs, blankets, baskets and boxes. Look at them and if any of them are similar to the ones owned by your kitten, write his name by them.

HOLIDAYS AND VISITS

Kittens usually stay at home, but sometimes they go on holiday or visits to people like Grandma and Grandpa. Here is a page on which you can record any trips away from home made by your own dear pet. You can record when Kitten went, where he went, whether he was carried in a basket or sat on someone's lap, whether he went by car, train, bus, and if he enjoyed the trip.

Date	Place	How carried	By whom	Transport	Did Kitten enjoy the trip?

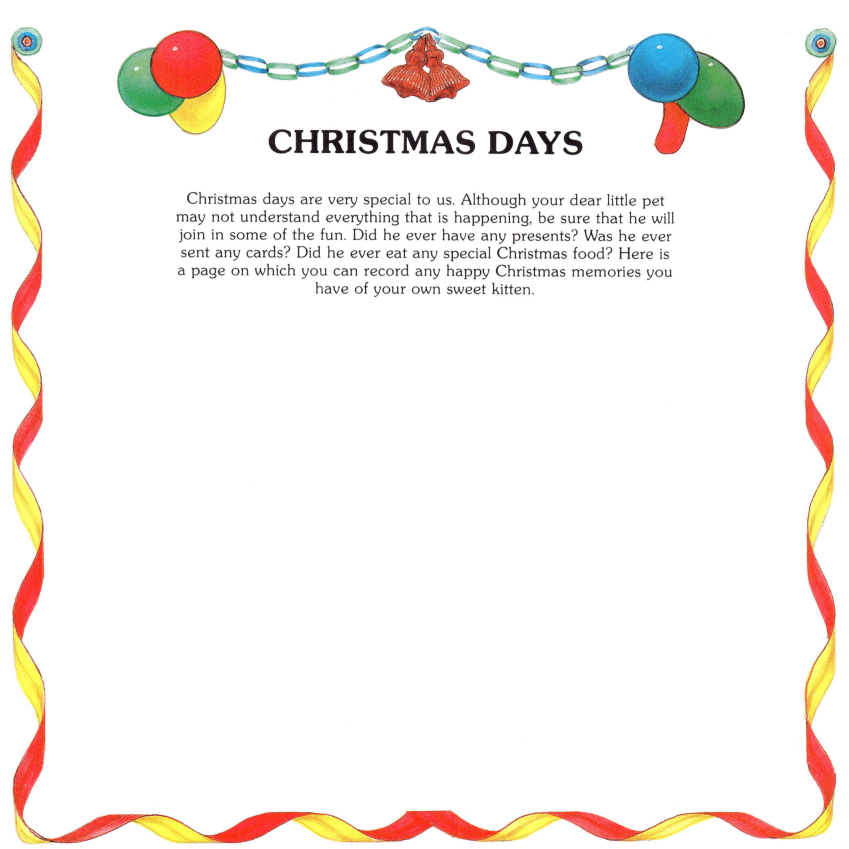

CHRISTMAS DAYS

Christmas days are very special to us. Although your dear little pet may not understand everything that is happening, be sure that he will join in some of the fun. Did he ever have any presents? Was he ever sent any cards? Did he ever eat any special Christmas food? Here is a page on which you can record any happy Christmas memories you have of your own sweet kitten.

BIRTHDAYS

The years roll by and soon your little bundle of furry fun will be a cat. Here are some pictures of lovely grown-up cats. Perhaps your kitten will become like one of them. On this page record any happy or funny memories you have of Kitten's birthdays. If there is nothing special to say, write the dates of the birthdays and some kisses to show how fond you are of your pet.